The Forward book of poetry
2004

The Forward book of poetry
2004

FORWARD
LONDON

First published in Great Britain by
Forward Ltd · 84–86 Regent Street · London W1B 5DD
in association with
Faber and Faber · 3 Queen Square · London WC1N 3AU

ISBN 0 571 22083 5 (paperback)

Compilation copyright © Forward Ltd 2003
Foreword copyright © Peter Stothard 2003
Front cover image by Will Scott

Reprographics by Zebra
Printed by Bath Press Ltd
Lower Bristol Road · Bath BA2 3BL · UK

A CIP catalogue reference for this book
is available at the British Library.

To Will Scott

Preface

AFTER TWELVE YEARS of the Forward Poetry Prizes, you might think it would be hard to summon up much enthusiasm for another year's collection. Not a bit of it. For poetry has an extraordinary ability, in Ezra Pound's words, to 'make it new', taking everyday words and giving them fresh life and meaning. Each year brings its own enchantments and surprises, in voices both familiar and relatively unknown.

One thing I find especially refreshing is that, despite regular predictions to the contrary, poetry continues to flourish. Far from being an ailing product of slim volumes and dusty shelves, poetry is all around us: perhaps more, today, than it has ever been before. For those who have eyes to see and ears to hear, it's in copywriting and greetings cards, in rap music and chart hits, in reading groups and pubs, bookshops and libraries and, of course, right here.

Poetry, after all, is one of our oldest art forms. It's also, arguably, one of our strongest, and the range, the number of entries and the number of different publishers involved in this year's collection all go to show that poetry remains a thriving industry. As much as anything else, *The Forward book of poetry* is a celebration of our vibrant poetry scene. I am grateful to our judges this year – Connie Bensley, Daisy Goodwin, Vona Groarke and Beth Orton, headed by Sir Peter Stothard – for their time and endeavours in sifting, rejecting and championing to reach their admirable shortlists.

As always, this book would not have appeared without the generous help of many people, and I'd like to thank everyone involved, not least Felix Dennis; Jeffery Tolman and Tim Baxter at Tolman Cunard; Gary McKeone and his team at the Arts Council of England; Jules Mann and her team at the Poetry Society; Dotti Irving, Liz Sich and Sophie Rochester at Colman Getty; our partners at Faber and Faber and the BBC; and, as always, everyone at Forward.

William Sieghart

Foreword

AFTER ABOUT AN HOUR we find a battlefield:
>   where opium-smokers doze among the Persian rugs,
>   and spies and whores in dim-lit snugs
>   discuss the failing prowess of the Allied powers.

We are not in Qatar or Kuwait, or even in the lesser known parts of
Whitehall. We are not in this year's eastern war. We are not even in a
war at all. We are in the meeting to pick the shortlist of would-be
winners for the Forward Poetry Prizes, an occasion which, while
exhibiting some of the panoply of battle, takes place this year without
too much loss of blood.

We are in the midst of Ciaran Carson's cycle of war-correspondent
poems, *Breaking News*, where the aftermath for civilians is almost as
grim as the battle itself:
>   a consignment of cavalry sabres was found
>   amid the ruins, fused into the most fantastic shapes
>   looking like an opium-smoker's cityscape
>   or a crazy oriental fairground.

As usual, someone likes this a lot. Someone else likes it less. That is
what happens when poets and critics get together to give marks to works
of sex, drugs and struggle which were never intended to be marked, only
to be read. But, in this year of Bush, Blair and Saddam, we are, at least
briefly, taken up and beyond our white table piled with books and
scorecards, out to somewhere truly bloodstained – to Gallipoli, the
Crimea, the sights seen by Florence Nightingale and William Howard
Russell, the horror that we made earlier.

Carson's vivid poem of victory and defeat came from one of the five
books which we chose to represent the best collections of the year.
It was one of many that were written before the dramas of March and
April 2003 but which spoke strongly to what was happening around
us as we judged. Lavinia Greenlaw's *Minsk* would have been gripping
at any time. But at a heightened, harassed, angry time, its grip was
harder still.

I read many of this year's poems while doing a prose writer's
journalist job of watching the Iraq war from Downing Street. So while
the American shortlisted poet, Billy Collins, was rejecting 'the three-

legged easel of realism' and decrying those who 'make the reader climb over the many fences of a plot', I was sitting, reading, waiting for the next appearance by the ministers of the War Cabinet or their celebrated Communicator in Chief, Alastair Campbell.

Every day there were new poems to read as well as new things to see. On the dark leather chairs between the front door of Number 10 and the corridor to the Campbell suite, it was amusing, almost helpful, to read Ian Duhig's strictures on the failings of prophetic texts. 'So DAM means SadDAM (why not NostraDAMus?)', he asks in one of the works, from the year 2000, brought together in his book *The Lammas Hireling*, named after his chilling National Poetry Competition winner. Duhig is a man of many voices, a magical storyteller, a poet who knows all the tricks to ensure that his message is heard. His professional work was once for the benefit of the homeless in London and the north of England. He still leads his readers along a wavy line where the public and private meet, puzzling all this year's panel with his three-word 'Canon' (Barrel./ Shot fish.), but ingeniously pleasing us too.

Forward judges are always too modest to declare that their own work is a public service. But we could make a good claim. Poetry is not a pretty sight *en masse*. Even the most devoted reader might pale at the piles of stapled card, shrink-wrapped multimedia confections and padded envelopes, in every one of which we seek and hope for something good. Day by day we pick through the boxes, desperate not to be dulled by excess but despairing too that, if we work too slowly, the work will never be done.

The prize for Best First Collection is a particular case for caution. The judges spent as long this year in choosing those whose poems we little knew as on those whose work we knew so well. It is not so difficult to find a Best Collection place for Paul Muldoon's latest slabs of 'dark matter', which this year include domestic tragedy as well as crimes that hide behind the battlefields of the twentieth century. 'The Stoic', from his *Moy Sand and Gravel* would stand out on the table of almost any prize jury – in any place or time. But we had to fight both each other's choices and our own prejudgements to find the works which will be collections for collectors in the future – or so we hope. Congratulations to (this is the moment for strict alphabetical order) Rhian Gallagher, A B Jackson, John McAuliffe, Jane Routh and Sarah Wardle.

During our decorous skirmishes, we asked ourselves whether there was any pattern to the poetry of the year beyond that which later events imposed, or at least imposed upon me. If I have learnt nothing else from my stint as chairman, I have learnt not to speak in any detail for my colleagues. We never quite reached the point of those protesters who hung 'Not In MY Name' banners around Downing Street. We haggled, traded and agreed. The choice is in all our names. But it is better not to explain too much. In any case, there was little agreement on any shape that could be seen in all that we had read, whether there was any theme among the pieces of West Indian patois, post-parturition therapy, pop-star wannabeing and rural mud and grime. There seemed to some of us to be an unusual number of foxes, though few as shimmering and slyly sniffing as Robert Minhinnick's Reynard who runs through the National Museum of Wales.

There seemed to me to be a dangerous absence of reading among the learning writers. No judge opening the latest parcel of volumes wants to find book after book by miniature Heaneys, minor Muldoons or followers of Fuller. But some greater sense that the newer poets were absorbing lessons from the giants of our day would be reassurance of continuing traditions of writing, not just the continuous desire to write.

Peter Stothard

Publisher Acknowledgements

Annemarie Austin · WHAT MY DOUBLE WILL · *Back from the Moon* · Bloodaxe
    Books

Kate Bass · THE ALBATROSS · *The Pasta Maker* · Smith/Doorstop Books

Judi Benson · BURYING THE ANCESTORS · Acumen

Ciaran Carson · THE WAR CORRESPONDENT · *Breaking News* · Gallery Press

Billy Collins · CREATURES · BY A SWIMMING POOL OUTSIDE SIRACUSA ·
    Nine Horses · Picador

Chris Considine · FEMALE COMPLAINT · *Learning to Look* · Peterloo Poets

David Constantine · SUBMERGED SITE · Dreamcatcher Books

Julia Copus · IN DEFENCE OF ADULTERY · *In Defence of Adultery* · Bloodaxe Books

Robert Crawford · FERRARI · *The Tip of My Tongue* · Cape Poetry

Annie Deppe · WALKING GLEN WEST · *Sitting in the Sky* · Summer Palace Press

Peter Didsbury · OWL AND MINER · *Scenes from a Long Sleep* · Bloodaxe Books

Ian Duhig · GLASS TALK · TAKING MY MEASURE · *The Lammas Hireling* · Picador

Richard Evans · PUBLIC DEATH · *The Zoo Keeper* · Egg Box Publishing

U A Fanthorpe · A MINOR ROLE · *Queuing for the Sun* · Peterloo Poets

Rhian Gallagher · EMBRACE · FIND A PARTNER · *Salt Water Creek* ·
    Enitharmon Press

Lavinia Greenlaw · SPIN . LUPINS · *Minsk* · Faber and Faber

Sophie Hannah · GOD'S ELEVENTH RULE · *First of the Last Chances* · Carcanet

Jean Harrison · WOMAN ON THE MOON · The North

Geoff Hattersley · TWO LOVE POEMS · *Harmonica* · Wrecking Ball Press

Brian Henry · INTRO TO LIT · *American Incident* · Salt Publishing

Ramona Herdman · SHE SPEAKS IN HER SLEEP · *Come What You Wished For* ·
    Egg Box Publishing

A B Jackson · FILING · THE SILKEN ROAD · *Fire Stations* · Anvil Press

Martha Kapos · MY NIGHTS IN CUPID'S PALACE · *My Nights in Cupid's Palace* ·
    Enitharmon Press

Gwyneth Lewis · MOTHER TONGUE · *Keeping Mum* · Bloodaxe Books

John McAuliffe · THE SCHOLAR'S VOYAGE · ACTION · *A Better Life* · Gallery Press

Contents

Shortlisted Poems
The Forward Prize for Best Collection

Ciaran Carson

THE WAR CORRESPONDENT

1
Gallipoli

Take sheds and stalls from Billingsgate,
glittering with scaling-knives and fish,
the tumbledown outhouses of English farmers' yards
that reek of dung and straw, and horses
cantering the mewsy lanes of Dublin;

take an Irish landlord's ruinous estate,
elaborate pagodas from a Chinese Delftware dish
where fishes fly through shrouds and sails and yards
of leaking ballast-laden junks bound for Benares
in search of bucket-loads of tea as black as tin;

take a dirty gutter from a back street in Boulogne,
where shops and houses teeter so their pitched roofs meet,
some chimney stacks as tall as those in Sheffield
or Irish round towers,
smoking like a fleet of British ironclad destroyers;

take the garlic-oregano-tainted arcades of Bologna,
linguini-twists of souks and smells of rotten meat,
as labyrinthine as the rifle-factories of Springfield,
or the tenements deployed by bad employers
who sit in parlours doing business drinking *Power's*;

then populate this slum with Cypriot and Turk,
Armenians and Arabs, British riflemen
and French Zouaves, camel-drivers, officers, and sailors,
sappers, miners, Nubian slaves, Greek money-changers,
plus interpreters who do not know the lingo;

dress them in turbans, shawls of fancy needlework,
fedoras, fezzes, sashes, shirts of fine Valenciennes,
boleros, pantaloons designed by jobbing tailors,
knickerbockers of the ostrich and the pink flamingo,
sans-culottes, and outfits even stranger;

requisition slaughter-houses for the troops,
and stalls with sherbet, lemonade, and rancid lard for sale,
a temporary hospital or two, a jail,
a stagnant harbour redolent with cholera,
and open sewers running down the streets;

let the staple diet be green cantaloupes
swarming with flies washed down with sour wine,
accompanied by the Byzantine
jangly music of the cithara
and the multi-lingual squawks of parakeets –

O landscape riddled with the diamond mines of Kimberley,
and all the oubliettes of Trebizond,
where opium-smokers doze among the Persian rugs,
and spies and whores in dim-lit snugs
discuss the failing prowess of the Allied powers,

where prowling dogs sniff for offal beyond
the stench of pulped plums and apricots,
from which is distilled the brandy they call 'grape-shot',
and soldiers lie dead or drunk among the crushed flowers –
I have not even begun to describe Gallipoli.

4
Balaklava

The Turks marched in dense columns, bristling with steel.
Sunlight flashed on the polished barrels of their firelocks
their bayonets, relieving their sombre hue,
for their dark blue uniforms looked quite black
when viewed *en masse*. The Chasseurs d'Afrique,
in light powder-blue jackets, with white cartouche belts, scarlet
pantaloons, mounted on white Arabs, caught the eye
like a bed of flowers scattered over the valley floor.

Some, indeed, wore poppies red as cochineal,
plucked from the rich soil, which bore an abundance of
     hollyhocks,
dahlias, anemones, wild parsley, mint, whitethorn, rue,
sage, thyme, and countless other plants whose names I lack.
As the Turkish infantry advanced, their boots creaked
and crushed the springy flowers, and delicate
perfumes wafted into the air beneath the April sky:
the smell of sweating men and horses smothered by flora.

Waving high above the more natural green
of the meadow were phalanxes of rank grass, marking the
     mounds
where the slain of October 25th had found their last repose,
and the snorting horses refused to eat those deadly shoots.
As the force moved on, more evidences of that fatal day
came to light. The skeleton of an English horseman
had tatters of scarlet cloth hanging to the bones of his arms;
all the buttons had been cut off the jacket.

Round as shot, the bullet-skull had been picked clean
save for two swatches of red hair. The remains of a wolfhound
sprawled at his feet. From many graves, the uncovered bones
of the tenants had started up, all of them lacking boots.

Tangled with rotted trappings, half-decayed horses lay
where they'd fallen. Fifes and drums struck up a rataplan;
so we swept on over our fellow men-at-arms
under the noon sun in our buttoned-up jackets.

Billy Collins

CREATURES

Hamlet noticed them in the shapes of clouds,
but I saw them in the furniture of childhood,
creatures trapped under surfaces of wood,

one submerged in a polished sideboard,
one frowning from a chair-back,
another howling from my mother's silent bureau,
locked in the grain of maple, frozen in oak.

I would see these presences, too,
in a swirling pattern of wallpaper
or in the various greens of a porcelain lamp,
each looking so melancholy, so damned,
some peering out at me as if they knew
all the secrets of a secretive boy.

Many times I would be daydreaming
on the carpet and one would appear next to me,
the oversize nose, the hollow look.

So you will understand my reaction
this morning at the beach
when you opened your hand to show me
a stone you had picked up from the shoreline.

'Do you see the face?' you asked
as the cold surf circled our bare ankles.
'There's the eye and the line of the mouth,
like it's grimacing, like it's in pain.'

'Well, maybe that's because it has a fissure
running down the length of its forehead
not to mention a kind of twisted beak,' I said,

taking the thing from you and flinging it out
over the sparkle of blue waves
so it could live out its freakish existence
on the dark bottom of the sea

and stop bothering innocent beachgoers like us,
stop ruining everyone's summer.

By a Swimming Pool Outside Siracusa

All afternoon I have been struggling
to communicate in Italian
with Roberto and Giuseppe who have begun
to resemble the two male characters
in my *Italian for Beginners*,
the ones always shopping, eating,
or inquiring about the times of trains.

Now I can feel my English slipping away,
like chlorinated water through my fingers.

I have made important pronouncements
in this remote limestone valley
with its trickle of a river.
I stated that it seems hotter
today even than it was yesterday
and that swimming is very good for you,
very beneficial, you might say.
I also posed burning questions
about the hours of the archaeological museum
and the location of the local necropolis.

But now I am alone in the evening light
which has softened the white cliffs,
and I have had a little gin in a glass with ice
which has softened my mood or –
how would you say in English –
has allowed my thoughts to traverse my brain
with greater gentleness, shall we say,

or, to put it less literally,
this drink has extended permission
to my mind to feel – what's the word? –
a friendship with the vast sky
which is very – give me a minute – very blue
but with much great paleness
at this special time of day, or as we say in America, now.

Ian Duhig

Glass Talk

She used such words as 'whimsey', 'ponty', 'cullet' ... and it intrigued
Mr Carpenter. Never had he met a woman who could talk glass before.
    The Glass Virgin, *Catherine Cookson*

With the last rack forked into the annealing kilns,
The time freed before the next contracted stint
Was spent on exhibition pieces or Christmas gifts:
The blowing irons became their own trumpets, raising

Poems from flint glass, a tall ship cast in water,
A bird from air, articulating rosary beads, all
Gathered and spun and tweaked from the fizzing light
And borax and cullet, then nursed at the glory-hole

As Catherine worshipped at the furnace of the word
But drew back from poetry, her first true romance,
Beating out the fluent rainbow of her paraison to prose's
Transparent panes, trimmed, squared off, filling shelves

As she bought libraries for the local university
To honour her with a calculatedly second-rank degree;
She who sent me questing for what poets most love,
To find the meanings of words, of words like 'graal'.

Taking My Measure

*Every decided colour does a certain violence to the eye and forces the organ
to opposition.*

    Goethe, Theory of Colours

Bet the last whistle you got fitted for was a 2-Tone Tonik?
Down the Palais giving it brown-gold brown-gold brown...
Oh. Funeral. Never mind, sir, I'll do you a second skin, an
Investment – be more of these from now on. Arms out, please.
Read any good books lately, sir? An anthology of German
    poetry?
OK. Not enough English? Oh yes, I've looked at some.
    Novalis?
A depressive mining engineer born during an eclipse of the sun,
His first and only love Sophie croaking before he could wurst
    her,
Of course he wrote hymns to the night and died of consumption,
That little black dress on every rack of sexy fatal illnesses,
A classic standby fall-back and drop-dead gorgeous accessorized
With a skimmed-milk-blue corsage and pre-existentialist bullshit
To set off the neo-Counter-Reformation revanchist
    thanatolatry –
'Unscorchable stands the Cross, victory banner of our faith!'
Did I mention that 'cretin' is French for 'Christian', sir?
I know for alchemists like him the Cross meant light, *ros crux*,
The dew cross, gold's solvent – we get all that old bollocks
Down the lodge. No one believes it. It's an excuse to get pissed
Like Rilke's alchemist – and Rilke? Done in by a poxy rose?
Want me to sew in a cosh-pocket in case you're jumped by
    tulips?
Just having a laugh, sir, just having a laugh. So what side do
You dress on, sir, or isn't that an issue for you any more?

Lavinia Greenlaw

SPIN
The Giraffe House, 1836

A cool exaggeration, five-metre doors
made reasonable with Roman arches.
An arrangement of parts, the giraffe
carries himself off, all height, no weight.

His ancestor arrived in London at the dawn
of transcendentalism and acetylene.
Walking from the dock to Regent's Park,
he freaked at the sight of a cow in Commercial Road.

Fellow ungulates, they met in the year
of the Arc de Triomphe, *The Pickwick Papers*
and the birth of the state of Arkansas,
feats of design.

LUPINS

'That girl's uncomfortable just being inside
her own skin.' Wolves comforted me.
I grew up within earshot.

Their howls would climb the hill
like tall spikes of blue flowers,
as if the zoo's iron railings

had unfurled beneath their spell.
Traffic gets up across the canal.
Some slip through lights

like baby golden tamarin monkeys.
Others wait, baffled clownfish
behind glass.

Paul Muldoon

He opens the scullery door, and a sudden rush
of wind, as raw as raw,
brushes past him as he himself will brush
past the stacks of straw

that stood in earlier for Crow
or Comanche tepees hung with scalps
but tonight pass muster, row upon row,
for the foothills of the Alps.

He opens the door of the peeling-shed
just as one of the apple-peelers –
one of almost a score
of red-cheeked men who pare

and core
the red-cheeked apples for a few spare
shillings – mutters something about 'bloodshed'
and the 'peelers'.

The red-cheeked men put down their knives
at one and the same
moment. All but his father, who somehow connives
to close one eye as if taking aim

or holding back a tear,
and shoots him a glance
he might take, as it whizzes past his ear,
for another Crow, or Comanche, lance

hurled through the Tilley-lit
gloom of the peeling-shed,
were he not to hear what must be an apple split
above his head.

The Stoic

This was more like it, looking up to find a burlapped fawn
half-way across the iced-over canal, an Irish navvy who'd
    stood there for an age
with his long-tailed shovel or broad griffawn,
whichever foot he dug with showing the bandage

that saved some wear and tear, though not so much that
    there wasn't a leak
of blood through the linen rag, a red picked up nicely by
    the turban
he sported, those reds lending a little brilliance to the bleak
scene of suburban or – let's face it – *urban*

sprawl, a very little brilliance. This was more like the
    afternoon last March
when I got your call in St Louis and, rather than rave
as one might rant and rave at the thought of the yew
from Deirdre's not quite connecting with the yew from
    Naoise's grave,

rather than shudder like a bow of yew or the matchless
    Osage orange
at the thought of our child already lost from view
before it had quite come into range,
I steadied myself under the Gateway Arch

and squinted back, first of all, through an eyelet of bone
to a point where the Souris
had not as yet hooked up with the Assiniboine,
to where the Missouri

had not as yet been swollen by the Osage,
then ahead to where – let's face it – there are now *two* fawns
on the iced-over canal, two Irish navvies who've stood there
    for a veritable age
with their long-tailed shovels or broad griffawns.

Shortlisted Poems
The Felix Dennis Prize for Best First Collection

Rhian Gallagher

EMBRACE

Unshowered, wrestling with the sea still on our skin
when she catches me, mid-room, with a kiss.
Not a passing glance of lips, but her intended
till I press back against the wall
laughing, in a body-search pose
as ready as her to forget about dinner.

Once, in our first months, we headed down Christopher Street
starch wafting from an open laundry, the sound of a press
squeezing a line along a sleeve. We slipped
across the West Side Highway, out on the pier
pressing our faces to the fence to catch an air of sea,
distant Liberty. Winter sun pouring its heart out
over the Hudson, she stepped into me –
the cold became a memory
smudged under our winter coats.

Two guys stood on the far side of the pier
looking baffled, how long they'd been there
god knows. Gulping, knees undone, we surfaced like swimmers
and almost ran back up Christopher Street
laughing. We'd been gone an hour, the night had come
there were shelves of lights up and down the tall streets,
she was all over me. Everything had turned on.

FIND A PARTNER

Our teacher is waltzing across the lawn with Linda.
An extension cord loops from the window,
crosses the rose-beds. The music crackles

as if on waves from England.
'Watch my feet,' he shouts
as he circles the fire bush

brushing the strawberry tree. Linda looks airborne.
Our ballroom has a sky-blue roof, a tractor
ploughing across the horizon,
roses peel to the sun

as piano launches anew, crossing a sea of static
a rise and a fall and a boy
with a grip on my arm as if it were a baseball bat.
The feeling of being inside my body
arrives with this news – it's going to be difficult.

A B Jackson

FILING

Oncology Centre. Cast-iron cabinets
of case histories, fresh figures, a request
in triplicate for a 'marrow harvest'...
I picture a bumpkin surgeon, in a sweat,
sorting cells like apples into buckets.

Facts are sensitive here. I work my way
through bales of personal files (always 'cancer'),
my throat cracked by so much dusty paper.
Truth comes to light on X-ray:

someone's brain, a wrinkled slice of fruit;
the skull's bone, a phosphorescent hoop,
classified and coded. Someone who.

Dear X, whatever daily face you wear,
may you never falter, never flower.

THE SILKEN ROAD

I take the shoots of river willow,
supple, fashioned circle-wise
and fastened so. There is a code
of charms upon the Silken Road.

They say there is a queen, her crown
a nesting-place for each cocoon:
on hatching, teams of busy worms
spin out, spin out the Silken Road.

To reach the journey's origin
brings riches… By this legend struck
so many homes stand empty. Miles
are posted on the Silken Road

by bones, some spread, some figuring
their common frames. That's animal,
that's other. All my brothers left
provisioned for the Silken Road,

and as I walk I scan the ground
for charcoal, tent-pegs, human tracks.
The light arches at my back
as night falls on the Silken Road.

My dream is short: a river lined
with willow, on its banks a queen
worm-eaten. There's myself grown old,
at home upon the Silken Road.

John McAuliffe

THE SCHOLAR'S VOYAGE

Tuesday, rain general, twelve years at his desk
And not a word put to paper. He took up his biro:
'I will walk out of this damp silent bungalow,
Up this street of cornerboys and unschooled know-alls,
Away from this city of "illitrate sleeveens" and "nice old
   misfortunes",
I will walk, biro upheld like a flag, out of this ex-country

'And I'll keep walking till a man stops me to ask:
"Where are you going with that small useless-looking oar?"
And right there and then I will bury this biro,
Under the dune grass, the blind worms, the sand and seashells
And I will live there, hooking fish, making nets and my fortune
Between the blue sky and the green sea.'

ACTION

It is 3 a.m., on a wet night, and I'm stood
In the middle of a field,
Listening to *The Open Mind*, a repeat, on a walkman
When Corman with his wand and loudspeaker cone
Directs me, 'Hey you', and then the long arm,
To walk across the field,
And to wade into the river
With the boom close to the water.
This is experience and I need experience.

Jane Routh

Signal Flag K: I wish to communicate with you

Kilo

Evenings, we sit on the rocks above the bay
and watch the tides. If there are signs
of a good sunset, take a jacket and an apple.
A nod might say *the buzzard's back
on the fence post*, a small gesture
question a dark streak in the waves.
Neither of us has anything to say
significant enough to break the silence.
I think I like low springs best,
the whole bay an emptied bowl,
the uncaught moment of the turn.

In the winter we shall drag the armchairs
nearer the stove, light all the lamps
and read each other
poems we do not understand
in case sound speaks for itself.
We can take turns to fetch tea and oranges.
No one comes out here till spring.

When I live alone again and am used to fears
at night when sheep rub up against the walls
I might remember scraps of old tunes;
I might remember singing in the bath.
Wrapped in white towels I shall stare out
through my reflection at the dark sea
for red lights half a mile off, find
a faint deck-light with binoculars
and watch the night-work of tiny figures.

THE FOOT THING

On your first visit, you put your feet up
on my polished table. Ankles crossed.
Doc Martens. (And this was years after
they were out of fashion with the young.)

It can't have been easy
for a small woman like you
to have kept your feet up like that.
I had to talk to you by leaning round.

I didn't know what to do –
whether to push them off, offer a cushion,
tell you I couldn't see you for your feet,
or ask if you had trouble with circulation.

I did the sort of thing I always do:
I just set a knife on one side
and a fork on the other as if that were
a customary greeting for soles

and kept my face blank.
It must have been a test, because
I never saw you do it again, not here,
not at home, not in a waiting room.

You came again so many times
I must have passed, though
feel I failed: I still don't know
what you wanted me to do.

Sarah Wardle

Poets' Parliament

Suppose poets stood for Parliament,
that they ran as Independent candidates,
canvassing streets on council estates
with poems printed on cards which said,
'Sorry you were out when I called.'
Suppose they read in village halls
to one man and a dog. Suppose they formed a party
and romped home with a landslide victory,
that after the General Election,
their maiden speeches were their first collections.

Imagine they took their seats in the Chamber,
resting their feet on its benches' green leather,
whilst at the Despatch Box the Junior Minister
for Sonnets held forth on the merits of metre,
as 'Order! Word order!' was called by the Speaker.
Imagine the Gallery full of Strangers,
recognising bards from Panorama,
or interviews held on College Green
about their favourite poems for the News at Ten.
Imagine poets' statues in Parliament Square
to Pope and Cope, or Ted and Sylvia.

Picture poets pacing the Committee Corridor,
composing a line instead of toeing one,
or seated at tables in the Tea Room alone,
scribbling on envelopes which bear the portcullis.
Picture them sipping Pimms on the Terrace,
with memos in verse circulating in Ministries,
along with rhymed soundbites on Government policies.
Picture poets of the past, now in the canon,
kicked up to the Lords, like Elysium,
as if the dead had wandered over

from across the road in Poets' Corner
to sit in ermine robes, day-dreaming,
still able to influence a Second Reading.

And suppose that in Central Lobby the Saints
for England, Scotland, Ireland and Wales were replaced
with Dylan Thomas over one arch, above another Yeats,
over the third arch William Shakespeare,
and Burns above the last which leads to the bar.

IF NATURE

If I were other than I find I am,
not atoms with this body and this face,
but scattered particles, part of the land,
the sea, the air, having left no trace
of what I was before, or who, or why,
as I shall be when I am turned to dust,
then I'd not be afraid to sleep or die,
trusting that of all gods Nature knows best.
If she gives me to winds, flames, streams and mud,
my dreams will bear fruit, my ideas come to bud.

If Nature were my beneficiary,
and I bequeathed to her all that I knew,
all that I did and was, am and shall be,
then like a treasury, her revenue
would be gathered together on collection day.
As scales tip down, so her bowl would fill,
while mine was emptied. My last breath would pay
her back the debt I owe. I'd foot the bill.
The lease on life I signed in blood would cease.
My dwelling would be let to someone else.

If I were melted down, like liquid gold
from solid ingots, to be turned to coin,
or sown like seeds in the autumnal cold,
so that in warmer weather from my groin,
my breasts, my hands, my lips, sprang up the shoots
of plum, of pear, of apple and of peach,
from my heart an oak tree spread its roots,
and from my liver lilac branches reached,
then there'd be nothing left of me to doubt her.
I myself would become the answer.

Shortlisted Poems
The Tolman Cunard Prize for Best Single Poem

Judi Benson

BURYING THE ANCESTORS

I
I'm tired of being crooned with the tune
of old Aunt Liza's dead goose,
lullabyed in those cotton fields back home,
roused to Dixie, swamped in the Sewanee River,
hearing Mammy say *hush chile*,
you know your Mamma was born to die.
The one they called Morning, born into the light,
taking her mamma's life. *Hush chile. Hush Mammy.*

I want the repeat names to stop repeating,
all those Henry fathers, greats and grands,
uncles, brothers, cousins intertwined, intermarried.
Juniors, Seniors, and all those Roman numerals, just delete.

Set fire to the tissue-thin letters of fine penmanship
and not much to say, *weather's fine,*
coming home in the covered wagon.
Clip the stamps, give them to the collector,
then burn baby burn.

Burn all their blusterings, their justifications for
blistering others' skin in the relentless summer heat,
while they wrapped themselves around shady porches.

I know to honour this blood flowing through me
is to say nothing. Don't mention the wills
begetting slaves and all their increase, forever, amen.
Sadie, Cicely, Moses, Caesar, and the one they called Patience.
Chains around their necks, chains around their ankles,
chains around their hopeless hearts,
all for the increase of those who refused to work the land,
whose hands were forbidden to touch dirt.

But my tongue wants to be released from its stays.
All those big hats bouncing with flowers, tossed in the wind,
pale faces unveiled, finding a trace of the darker hue hinted at.

II
Let Eugenia in her ball gown go waltzing
back out the door. Stop fanning her lashes at the Judge,
begging him to pass the Secession Act on her birthday.
Pretty please Judge, I'll be 19. And so he did,
slicing Georgia off from the Union.

And then what, and what if only Johnny
had come marching home again.
Eugenia, dead of night, bundling her babies
into the flat wagon, crossing the rising river,
just before the bridge gave out,
whipping the horses and cursing those damn Yankees
she'd never forgive, nor all her increase.

Eugenia always seen in mourning-black,
burying her father, her babies, her husband.
Rocking on her porch, silver-haired,
a black ribbon round her neck, glint in her eye,
sure the South would rise again.

III
Soft people, hard people, lines crissing and crossing
the economic divide, rattling at the edges of china cups,
hands cracked from hard work, soft hands slipping into gloves.
Ladies and Gents, rebels and ruffians.

These strangers: Benjamin, Lydia, Josh and Jasmine,
flattened in the black and white photograph,
sitting stiffly, even when casual,
suspicious of the man under black cloth
the little box with the sudden *Pop*!
Smile? Say cheese? What's that.

Meat? No one's had any in months.
Cracked corn, bucked wheat,
and always hoe cake, though once
it was told, syrup.

Once the land was fertile.
Then grew to be like its people, over-worked, exhausted,
tobacco, cotton, corn, thirsty for rain.
The great greats and not-so-greats
with their sharp pulled back hair,
tight knots, tributaries of trouble
running across their faces,
bending their mouths down,
bones edging through the little skin.
Even the old-eyed children
clench an angry desperation in their faces.

Left-overs, that was all some could afford to rent.
All they had, they'd inherited, the feather bed,
one scrawny mule, three slaves and all their increase.
Just another mouth to feed. Amen.

IV
Planters, plantation owners, preachers, politicians,
doctors, lawyers, artists, teachers, n'er do wells, drunks,
do-gooders, glamour girls posing for Coca Cola ads:
Camille, Vally, Lamar,
naughty girls seen smoking in public, racey women,
swell men, bootleg whisky, speakeasys, suicides,
insanity, vanity and humility. Anecdotes and ancient history,
all it boils down to. Stories told, changed in the telling.

Henry was driving through the back roads in his Model T,
so fast he killed a bunch of chickens on the dusty Georgia clay.
Hey Mister, you gotta pay, shouts the irate farmer.
How much? Make it fifteen dollars.
Here's 30, cause I'm coming back just as fast.

Little Henry, Big Henry, dead Henry.

Some lost to sea, some to land. War heroes,
influenza victims, gamblers, ladies' men,
loose women, tight-laced Baptists, Huguenots,
shouting Methodists,
Klan members and abolitionists,
suffragettes and Southern Belles,
side by side now, bones mouldering together,
mixing up the arguments, leaving all that love hanging.

V
They were just people, sugah, father said,
they worked hard and were honest. Religious folk,
never played cards on Sunday, never mixed with coloreds.
Amen. Praise the Lord and pass the ammunition,
pass the succotash, pass the buck, cross yourself,
swear to tell the truth,
pray the Lord your soul to take
and all that hate: Absalom, Walter, Kitty, Caroline, Dolly
with the hole in her stocking, dance with her,
dance with all her dead. Jason with the hole in his head. Fix it.
The named and never named, the never talked about one
who ran away with the chauffeur, the older one who stayed,
the one forever missing in action,
the ones whose minds flew away.

VI
Go away then, I tell them. Stop your whispering in shadows,
plucking at my scalp, sucking at my conscience.
Half-words almost heard,
how my hands are too soft and my thinking too,
how we've all gone soft.

They puzzle over the flushing of the loo.
Wonder why we waste the rich soil
they gave their lives to,

growing flowers that bear no fruit.
Lena, Ezekiel, Liza, Jebediah.
Names without faces, faces without names.

Go back to Georgia, Kentucky, Tennessee, Maryland,
Virginia, up on over the border to Pennsylvania.
Go back over to the side you should have fought on,
change the colour of your uniform,
change your vote, change the fate, un-buy those slaves,
uncrack the cowhide, unlick your lips, that hunger
you have for black skin to lash, your tongue a weapon,
quoting the Good Book, washing your hands clean in holy water.

Leave the land to the Natives who know how to honour it.
Get back on that ship to England,
cross the channel back to France.
Take the Master out of Mister. Take off the H
you added to the family name. Return to your mother-tongue,
Parlez vous again in the city you came from,
before they chased you out, or the grass got greener,
before the drought, the flood,
before some great great named John
went down with the ship called Increase,
before the long bitter of it all got passed down,
before the going down to the frozen ground
of the one without a name.

Call her Peace and let her rest Amen.

David Constantine

SUBMERGED SITE

But the sea will not keep still. Down there
They fixed two lovers in marble tesserae
BC/AD. Peer through the boat's glass floor:
Some days they're as clear as you and me
In the mirror doing what lovers always do
And hope to do again together soon.

In roofless rooms, so long under the sea,
It makes a ceiling painting of us two
Flat out, peering down. They seem to be in the rooms
Of an old sonnet, pinned in place by rhymes
As hard as tesserae, in quatrains, line by line,
Mine and thine, oh my beloved, thou and I
Doing what we do and still a while longer will.

But how like us or unlike those two are
In looks today refuses to come clear.
Turbid water. The sea will not keep still.

Jean Harrison

Woman on the Moon

This is the longest night I've ever faced.
I'm putting it off while I write to you
watching blues creep up.

The earth has been huge in our sky all day
and as it sank, I felt I could reach out
and touch you, but all the time indigo
was seeping into the valley.
Now it's flooded and the hills
are like shadowed snow.

An hour ago we spoke by satellite.
You told me all you'd been doing.
I said I'd been X-raying moonrock
and you went quiet; that I'd been walking
and my footsteps would lie there always,
that there's no wind,
and you said, 'There must be.'

I said, 'The light that comes here from earth
is blue and I'm losing it. Nights here
are as long as fourteen days on earth,'
and you said, 'That doesn't make sense.'

It should soon be time for your father
to give you your supper and afterwards
both of you will go into the garden
but I'll be on the side of the moon
that's turning towards space.

Robert Minhinnick

THE FOX IN THE NATIONAL MUSEUM OF WALES

He scans the frames but doesn't stop,
this fox who has come to the museum today,
his eye in the renaissance
and his brush in the baroque.

Between dynasties his footprints
have still to fade, between the Shan and the Yung,
the porcelain atoms shivering at his touch,
ah, lighter than the emperor's breath, drinking rice wine from
   the bowl,
daintier than the eunuch pouring wine.

I came as quickly as I could
but already the fox had left the Industrial Revolution behind,
his eye has swept the age of atoms,
the Taj Mahal within the molecule.

The fox is in the folios and the fossils, I cry.
The fox is in photography and the folk studies department.
The fox is in the flux of the foyer,
the fox is in the flock.
The fox is in the flock.

Now the fox sniffs at the dodo
and at the door of Celtic orthography.
The grave-goods, the chariots, the gods of darkness,
he has made their acquaintance on previous occasions.

There, beneath the leatherbacked turtle he goes,
the turtle black as an oildrum,
under the skeleton of the whale he skedaddles,
the whalebone silver as bubblewrap.

Through the light of Provence moves the fox, through
the Ordovician era and the Sumerian summer,
greyblue the brush on him, this one who has seen so much,
blood on the bristles of his mouth,
and on his suit of iron filings the air fans like silk.

Through the cubists and the surrealists
This fox shimmies surreptitiously,
Past the artist who has sawn himself in half
under the formaldehyde sky
goes this fox shiny as a silver
fax in his fox coat,
for at a fox trot travels this fox
backwards and forwards in the museum.

Under the bells of brugmansia
that lull the Ecuadoran botanists to sleep,
over the grey moss of Iceland
further and further goes this fox,
passing the lambs at the feet of Jesus,
through the tear in Dante's cloak.

How long have I legged it
after his legerdemain, this fox
in the labyrinth, this fox that never hurries
yet passes an age in a footfall, this fox
from the forest of the portrait gallery
to engineering's cornfield sigh?

I will tell you this.
He is something to follow,
this red fellow.
This fox I foster –
he is the future.

No-one else
has seen him yet.
But they are closing
the iron doors.

Alison Prince

SPRING

There are no midges at this time of year.
The narcissi under the cherry tree
a business plan turn with the fluency
of dancers in the April wind, and where
the hyacinths unfurl beside the door
the scent is heavenly. *and we must all*
congratulate our When the blossoms fall
from the forsythia, I must make sure
to prune it straight away, so it will bloom
next spring. The thyme has spread a sweet carpet
over the paving stones *Our secretary gets*
her absent-minded moments.
Hell. The room
on this twelfth floor is waiting, all its eyes
turned and its lips pursed in impatient smiles.
I'm reading, breathless. I have fallen miles
out of my garden, to this place of sky.

Highly Commended Poems
2003

Annemarie Austin

WHAT MY DOUBLE WILL

My double will do it: go inside,
seek out the ward, not mind
when he lifts to her the blank eyes
of a bored stranger on the bus
who only notices you enough to
edge an inch nearer the window
when you must sit next to him.

My double will be jaunty, carry
fruitcake and daffodils maybe –
the brandy he used to like become
'impossible with the medication'.
She'll have expected that and
the way a tranquilliser's hammer
has rendered the fog she brings
even more a pea-souper for him.

My double won't care if he asks
about a job she never had in a town
she's never been to. She'll collaborate
when he tells how he piloted a plane
to Africa and back the night before,
killing the enemy all along the way –
so they lie in a swathe from Timbuktu
to Sidi Barani and beyond, let's say.

But I'll stand outside the hospital's
front glass wall like a cigar-store
Indian – wooden, transfixed. I'll carry
air and hold emptiness in my mouth.
And the horror I'm ashamed of will
wash over me like cold rain and wash
over me again, only my double gone in.

Kate Bass

THE ALBATROSS

When I know you are coming home
I put on this necklace:
glass beads on a silken thread,
a blue that used to match my eyes.
I like to think I am remembering you.
I like to think you don't forget.

The necklace lies heavy on my skin,
it clatters when I reach down
to lift my screaming child.
I swing her, roll her in my arms until she forgets.
The beads glitter in the flicker of a TV set
as I sit her on my lap
and wish away the afternoon.

I wait until I hear a gate latch lift
the turn of key in lock.
I sit amongst toys and unwashed clothes,
I sit and she fingers the beads until you speak
in a voice that no longer seems familiar, only strange.
I turn as our child tugs at the string.
I hear a snap and a sound like falling rain.

Chris Considine

Female Complaint

After a week of sulks I was glad to see the back of him
I had stopped asking if anything was wrong no point
he was probably hearing voices again Do this Do that
Go to Nineveh anyway he didn't go to Nineveh
because I heard him on the phone to the travel agent
I refrained from suggesting he should go back to work and make
some money instead of squandering it on boat trips
he packed his own suitcase and off he went in a bad temper
because he couldn't find his sunglasses then blissful
peace and quiet for a few days he wouldn't need
sunglasses I thought because the weather was terrible
for July every evening on the weathermap
there seemed to be a new low coming in
over the sea rain gales thunder the lot
served him right swanning off god knows where
the next thing was a phone call at three in the morning
the line was dreadful he'd fallen overboard been shipwrecked
one or the other lost his credit cards could I ring the bank
then it got really garbled he'd been in Wales
or he'd seen a whale he'd been swallowed
and vomited up on a beach I switched off I'm afraid
and let him ramble said Really or Oh dear
or Mmm whenever there was a silence I mean
there had been other episodes I thought of ringing
the doctor but I couldn't find out where Jonah was
he didn't seem to know himself the line went dead
I went back to sleep what was I supposed to do
a week later there was a card from Nineveh
how had he got there I wanted to know
it said glad you are not here so was I
I knew he would turn up eventually and he did
a ring at the front door late one evening he'd lost his keys
but after all that his mood didn't seem to have improved

he slammed the door stamped up the stairs demanded food
I never did get to the bottom of it it's no use asking
I wouldn't get a straight answer and he's still
not back at work though thank goodness he's found
a hobby that gets him out from under my feet
now he spends most of the day in his greenhouse
which is fine as long as his plants are doing all right
life isn't worth living when something fails to thrive
talk about weeping and wailing men are such children
I just switch off and say Yes dear No dear Write to
Gardeners' Question Time I can't be doing with it.

Julia Copus

IN DEFENCE OF ADULTERY

We don't fall in love: it rises through us
the way that certain music does –
whether a symphony or ballad –
and it is sepia-coloured,
like spilt tea that inches up
the tiny tube-like gaps inside
a cube of sugar lying by a cup.
Yes, love's like that: just when we least
needed or expected it
a part of us dips into it
by chance or mishap and it seeps
through our capillaries, it clings
inside the chambers of the heart.
We're victims, we say: mere vessels,
drinking the vanilla scent
of this one's skin, the lustre
of another's eyes so skilfully
darkened with bistre. And whatever
damage might result we're not
to blame for it: love is an autocrat
and won't be disobeyed.
Sometimes we manage
to convince ourselves of that.

Robert Crawford

Student poser, Presbyterian swami,
When Being and Nothingness ruled the Kelvin Way,

I rebelled by carrying a rolled umbrella
To lectures. I never finished *La Nausée*.

Chaperoned through suburbs by my virginity,
My act of Existential Choice was pie,

Beans and chips at Glasgow's boil-in-the-bag
Student Ref. Couscous? I'd rather have died.

Nightlife was homelife, the tick-tock soothe
Of a bowling club clock, long darning needles' hint

Of suture, so homely and sharp;
Each birthday, a wrapped after-dinner mint.

So, years later, graduated to the glassy Minch,
On the Castlebay ferry, leaning over its rail

Where, below us, a harnessed sailor
Sang from a cradle, painting the ship as it sailed,

I knew, stroking your breasts beneath your blouse,
Both being and nothingness. We kissed like a cashless king

And queen who've just splashed out and bought
A Ferrari for the first day of spring.

Annie Deppe

Walking Glen West

I couldn't say what longing
rose up in me as I climbed

the faint path towards the Bullig,
evening light hammering

the hillside golden. First
heather of the year, small bright globes

mixing with the gorse's thorny yellow
and the susurration

of long-stemmed grasses, purple,
flowing beside the path which keeps

rising above green harbour waters.
I found, as I followed dried cattle prints

and sought footholds on steep ledge faces,
something inside was pressing up.

Even before I reached the cliffs
at the island's shoulder with their early

summer spread of yellow trefoils,
sea pinks waving, even before

the skylark's song spiralled upwards,
something was making itself felt:

watching the long waves sweep in
I realized my father has come

and wrapped himself around this island.
So many years since his death.

So many years since I threw earth
into his grave and willed him to stay

buried. While I sat high above the sea
and watched, far out, a red boat rock,

while I sat near the graves
of drowned sailors, their heads and feet

marked by field stones, buried in sight
of where they washed ashore,

I realized I've reached the age
my father was the summer he spent

drowning. I was six, he took me out to fish
as he foundered in his own dark waters,

could not find the air he needed.
This morning, when I saw pink-grey fish

in North Harbour, I recalled how he'd rent a boat
and row to the end of Roseland Lake

where we'd drift on weedy waters
and pull pumpkin fish, one flat orange body

after another, and then, too bony to eat,
throw them back again. All about our boat –

am I remembering this right? –
little dead suns with unthinking eyes.

One steamy August afternoon,
we children were sent to wait

on the back-porch swing while the doctor came
and stole our real father away.

I wish in some ways he'd died that day,
spared us those years of fear and anger.

If you make your father mad, you will kill him.
When Daddy's raging face loomed

above me, I turned and ran.
It took him thirty years to die.

Waves gather and hurdle over jagged
rocks half-submerged beneath the sea.

Up here, the rough yellow light
of curled lichen threads. What surprises me

after all this time is that something in me
is softening. Recently, I'm remembering

curling up in his lap, and how
his hearing aid – the old one

clipped to the top of his undershirt –
squealed and made us laugh.

How he'd cut an apple in half, show me
the star of Bethlehem hidden within.

Late sun slides into cloud banks
above the mainland's mountains,

black-backed gulls ride currents
and swallows dip and swoop. Once

I watched fireworks with my parents
by the Quinebaug River. Chrysanthemums

filled the air, but my youngest son,
frightened by the noise, began to cry.

His grandfather, so often
lacking patience, lifted him onto his lap,

tucked Michael's head beneath
his jacket flap to muffle the sound.

How is it that anger and love can be
wrapped so tightly against our hearts?

Held close like that
against his grandfather's chest,

a place of warmth and darkness,
Michael calmed, then burrowed part way out

until, ears still sheltered, he could peer up
into the coloured night.

I must have once been held
that way myself. My father must have been

a tent, spread out against the sky.

Peter Didsbury

OWL AND MINER

The owl alights on his shoulder.
All the day-shift she's waited patiently there,
high in the pine that grows hard by the pit-head.
Waited blinking and dreaming,
and turning the slow escutcheon of her face.
Waited as that which would serve to draw her master
back with songs from his deep Plutonic shades.

Thus it is that he steps from the earth and is greeted.
She furls her wings, and as they set off
on their mile up the darkening lane,
towards the low-banked cloud of the clustering houses,
he starts to sing to her. I see his white smoke.
His breath on the air he casts as if he would net
the voices of ghosts in the empty elder trees.
For it is winter now, and his songs are of winter.
Wind unparcelled across the keen land.
First light snowfall turning black on hedge.
Warren and iron pool and far road-end,
where now the yellow lights begin to come on,
in twos and threes, haltingly, as if to conjure
the stars to commence their stammering nightly speech.

Richard Evans

Public Death

We march, we who were poor and lost sight of symposium,
We march through the streets and down the road by the park,
One in the blasé profundity – we will pass, we all drop –
Together, at last, in an old woman's box.

Liz, eighty-four, died last night in her sleep. How sad
To think of her arthritic flippers, her clumps,
And the full arm of her spine as she wriggled against
The teeth of death, with a half-hope, how sad.

A man in the Nag's Head gave his condolences,
I didn't recognise him. He had eaten twelve sandwiches.
He said, 'She was a great woman…' I said, 'No, she was a nan.'
He had one eye on the telly and asked, 'how's Charles bearing it?'

Queen Elizabeth the Queen Mother died the same day,
Our seven looked timid to a million and the excuses on the phone,
'Wouldn't Liz have wanted it?' and 'A funeral's a funeral,'
Dropped hard-faced onto a stained carpet.

Fifteen in total came to nudge the coffin with their goodbyes,
No one but my mother cried, and I do not think
They were all tears of love. But I wrote a poem
Called 'Remember That', slipped in a salmon

Or two for good measure. A blue-rinse sniffled
As I rhymed 'miss you' with 'tissue'
And the priest patted my back enthusiastically,
Said I could teach Mr Motion a thing. Still, I heard him

Talking about corgis at the reception, and my gran
Didn't have corgis, nor even a Jack Russell,

But she did have a large framed picture of Bertie,
The tabby who died three years before and stunk of piss.

– You loved that piss-stinking bastard.

So I remember what you said, when the dip of the six tongued
Tulip holds a moment's attention, when the elm all at once
Surprises me and the water is impossible permutation.
You said something that sounded alright, once.
But now you are dead.

You're not a symbol of what anyone feels
Nor what I feel, so see you, Gran, if it goes on.
Let's meet sometime, indifferently,
Over a few biscuits, and a chat about the royals.

U A Fanthorpe

A MINOR ROLE

I'm best observed on stage,
Propping a spear or making endless
Exits and entrances with my servant's patter
Yes, sir. O no, sir. If I get
These midget moments wrong, the monstrous fabric
Shrinks to unwanted sniggers.

But my heart's in the unobtrusive
The waiting-room roles: driving to hospitals,
Parking at hospitals. Holding hands under
Veteran magazines; making sense
Of consultants' monologues; asking pointed
Questions politely; checking dosages,
Dates; getting on terms with receptionists;
Sustaining the background music of civility.

At home in the street you may see me
Walking fast in case anyone stops:
0, getting on, getting better my formula
For well-meant intrusiveness.
                                   At home,
Thinking ahead: *Bed? A good idea!*
(Bed solves a lot); answer the phone,
Be wary what I say to it, but grateful always;
Contrive meals for a hunger-striker; track down
Whimsical soft-centred happy-all-the-way-through novels;
Find the cat (mysteriously reassuring);
Cancel things, tidy things; pretend all's well,
Admit it's not.

Learn to conjugate all the genres of misery:
Tears, torpor, boredom, lassitude, yearnings
For a simpler illness, like a broken leg

* * *

Enduring ceremonial delays. Being referred
Somewhere else. Consultant's holiday. Saying *Thank you*
For anything to everyone
                              Not the star part.
And who would want it? I jettison the spear,
The servant's tray, the terrible drone of Chorus:
Yet to my thinking this act was ill-advised
It would have been better to die*. No it wouldn't!

I am here to make you believe in life.

*Chorus from Oedipus Rex, *trans E F Watling*

Sophie Hannah

GOD'S ELEVENTH RULE

I want to sit beside the pool all day,
Swim now and then, read *Peeping Tom*, a novel
By Howard Jacobson. You needn't pay
To hire a car to drive me to a hovel
Full of charred native art. Please can I stay
Behind? I will if necessary grovel.
I want to sit beside the pool all day,
Swim now and then, read *Peeping Tom*, a novel.

Pardon? You're worried I will find it boring?
My days will be repetitive and flat?
You think it would be oodles more alluring
To see the chair where Mao Tse Tung once sat.
Novels and pools are all I need for touring,
My *Peeping Tom*, *Nostromo* after that.
Pardon? You're worried I will find it boring.
My days will be repetitive and flat.

Okay, so you were right about *Nostromo*,
But I've a right to stay in this hotel.
Sienna: I refused to see *il duomo*.
(Does that mean Mussolini? Who can tell?)
In Spain I told them, 'Baño, bebo, como.'
I shunned the site where Moorish warriors fell.
Okay, so you were right about *Nostromo*
But I've a right to stay in this hotel.

I'm so alarmed, my voice becomes falsetto
When you prescribe a trip round local slums.
Would I drag you from Harvey Nicks to Netto?
No I would not. Down, down go both my thumbs.
I'm happy in this five-star rich man's ghetto
Where teeth are, by and large, attached to gums.

I'm so alarmed, my voice becomes falsetto
When you prescribe a trip round local slums.

It's not an English thing. No need to grapple
With the strange ways we foreigners behave.
My colleague would be thrilled to see your chapel,
Turrets and frescos and your deepest cave,
But as for me, I'd rather watch sun dapple
The contours of a chlorinated wave.
It's not an English thing. No need to grapple
With the strange ways we foreigners behave.

I want to spend all day beside the pool.
I wish that this were needless repetition,
But next to you, a steroid-guzzling mule,
A hunger strike and the first Christian mission
Look apathetic. God's eleventh rule:
Thou shalt get sore feet at an exhibition.
I want to spend all day beside the pool.
I wish that this were needless repetition.

Geoff Hattersley

Two Love Poems

(i) Younger, Fresher

I got my hair cut
this morning, too short
is how it looks to me
but she likes it, Jeanette.
She says it makes me look
younger, fresher.
She says it makes me look
as if I know I'm living a life
that could be
much worse.
'Do you like them?' she asks,
turning her feet this way and that
in some new black
high-heeled sandals.

(ii) Bed Poem

She holds me from behind
or I curl up to her,
I like to feel her warm
backside. Like a workman's
brazier, I tell her.
Go to sleep, she murmurs.

I'm sure someone once said
a poem should be like an
onion, peeling it, layer after layer
bringing tears to the eyes,
but who'd want to wake up
in bed with that person?

Brian Henry

INTRO TO LIT

He read a poem full of arrogance
and self-hatred. Called it 'My Misery'.
When the teacher asked the class
to describe the monster's misery,
a student declared *The monster's*
misery is that he is miserable. #9)
The monster is a creature but no
doctor; the doctor is a creature but
no monster. What proportion of the time
will a creature be a monster?: 1/2, 1/3,
1/4, none of the. Evaluations are due
by the end of the day, please be

Ramona Herdman

She speaks in her sleep in the birdsong creak
of an unoiled brass-wheeled hummingbird wound
for an emperor – a snickering, scales down the stairs,
sweet-pitched sound.

This small-timer found and swaddled and fed
for noises like this, that nest in my head
and sleep in my hand.
Clear as a ring in the plush of my heart.

To have and to hold
and to lie separate
and strain for her breath.

Yet if she left it, folded small by the cumulus sea.
If she swam small, wet-haired as a lemming,
off to the line of dark grey where the sky holds the sea
it wouldn't kill me.

She lies in her sleep or smiles or screams
tongue twisted tight round her sweet sweet dreams.

Martha Kapos

My Nights in Cupid's Palace

Down a narrow hall ending
in a drop of light,
velvet rooms lead
to velvet rooms. Silently the vivid food

appears again, well-lit, on tables laid
by hands without arms
lavish fingers without hands,

asking to be touched.
Help Yourself. My mouth is soft
as water, as I think – *Yes.*

Alone in this flimsy tent,
on the far edge of a field, my mind
an embryonic curl
grows very small until it goes out.

Gwyneth Lewis

Mother Tongue

'I started to translate in seventy-three
in the schoolyard. For a bit of fun
to begin with – the occasional "fuck"
for the bite of another language's smoke
at the back of my throat, its bitter chemicals.
Soon I was hooked on whole sentences
behind the shed, and lessons in Welsh
seemed very boring. I started on print,
Jeeves & Wooster, Dick Francis, James Bond,
in Welsh covers. That worked for a while
until Mam discovered Jean Plaidy inside
a Welsh concordance one Sunday night.
There were ructions: a language, she screamed,
should be for a lifetime. Too late for me.
Soon I was snorting Simenon
and Flaubert. Had to read much more
for any effect. One night I OD'd
after reading far too much Proust.
I came to, but it scared me. For a while
I went Welsh-only but it was bland
and my taste was changing. Before too long
I was back on translating, found that three
languages weren't enough. The "ch"
in German was easy, Rilke a buzz...
For a language fetishist like me
sex is part of the problem. Umlauts make me sweat,
so I need a multilingual man
but they're rare in West Wales and tend to be
married already. If only I'd kept
myself much purer, with simpler tastes,
the Welsh might be living...

Detective, you speak
Russian, I hear, and Japanese.
Could you whisper some softly?
I'm begging you. Please...'

Jamie McKendrick

Right of Way

Were we expecting these toads on our doorstep?
– the smaller with a jewel stuck
to her forehead, a round white pebble,
a third eye, only blind, without a pupil,
picked up on her pilgrimage beside
the artificial lake or risking the ringroad.

It's chill and blank, that stone – perhaps a chunk
of granite ballast from the virtual quarry,
the way it seems more of an ailment
than an ornament. Her mate is clad in
eco-warrior fatigues: grey chevrons
screenprinted on a ground of dull jade.

Both have a furtive, raddled air as if
in protest at the dust fumes and the din
as the grabclaw clanks on the wagons' rim,
loading and unloading ballast. But the door open,
they make for the hallway with sagging hops
like small encrusted beanbags on the move

and seem to know, thanks all the same,
where the back door is, like it was their
house, or no house at all – their right of way
from well before we'd made such strides ahead
as building walls to live inside of, theirs before
we'd dragged our pelts and selves out of the mud.

Lachlan McKinnon

ACQUAINTANCE

The river bank
was a white gash,
chalk spoil
from the new motorway.

I thought of you
in your estranged
apartness orbiting
a nowhere childhood.

We never met
then; seldom, later.
A rackety bar
in Earl's Court.

Sometimes affection
wants nothing bodily
or spiritual,
it's just there,

sudden as rain,
strong as rivers,
stubborn as reeds,
candid as chalk.

Andrew McNeillie

Now, Then

Wake early for an early start and softly
while the world sleeps tight go where

the first of day begins and dawn-light
throws a loop around the nursing air

of some old song you have to heart but
guard well that space between you and

the chorus and only to your self attend:
step up, now then, and sing undaunted.

Glyn Maxwell

The Snow Village

In the age of pen and paper,
when the page was a snow village,
when days the light was leafing through
descended without message,

the nib that struck from heaven
was the sight of a cottage window
lit by the only certain
sign of a life, a candle,

glimpsed by a stranger walking
at a loss through the snow village.
All that can flow can follow
that sighting, though no image,

no face appear – not even
the hand that draws across it –
though the curtains close the vision,
though the stranger end his visit,

though the snow erase all traces
of his passing through the village,
though his step become unknowable
and the whiteness knowledge.

Edwin Morgan

21 June

Fade then, light; but longing never will.
Midsummer makes the west spectacular
and even gives its last glow a show
of reluctance, as if it had postponed
midnight. But midnight is too faithful.
You're back among the black, the black,
you're down and fit to drown, to drown,
you're padding into nightmare town.
You haven't got a house, a bed-light,
there are no clocks or telephones out there,
you are on your own, you have a large panic
waiting to break through your chest, you are panting,
you count, as it arrives, each brimming pang.
What a clutch of sheets! What a parody of pain!

The longest day, the night is not so long.
You fling back the curtains, the morning sky
is like a meadow. What is it you want?
I don't know. You cannot walk there. No.
So what do you want? The morning, perhaps,
and then I want the day, another day.

Jenny Morris

INFANT IN THE STEPMOTHER'S GARDEN

The gate to the wood is chained
and lacquered fish mouth warnings.
Beyond the stile and cedars
his thistledown head is dwarfed by grass.
He follows yew roots sliding loose
in the purple shadows of topiary,
investigates ladybirds hunting
on the undersides of box leaves,
touches with his pale eyes
stone fruit dripping swags
of petrified foliage,
collects wooden roses of cones
and negotiates cobbles leading
to tiger lilies, acanthus spikes
and terracotta jars.

Inside the great hazel hedge
he is lost in darkness
below cypress sentinels.
Now his inquisitive smallness
must test the deep murk of the far lake
while on the empty croquet lawn
there is no thunk of mallets
to disturb the hot silence.

Stanley Moss

HEART WORK

No moon is as precisely round as the surgeon's light
I see in the center of my heart.
Dangling in a lake of blood, a stainless steel hook,
unbaited, is fishing in my heart for clots.
Across the moon I see a familiar dragonfly,
a certain peace comes of that. Then the dragonfly
gives death or gives birth to a spider it becomes –
they are fishing in my heart with a bare hook,
without a worm – they didn't even fish like that
when the Iroquois owned Manhattan.
Shall I die looking into my heart, seeing so little,
will the table I lie on become a barge, floating
endlessly down river, or a garbage scow?

There is a storm over the lake.
There are night creatures about me:
a Chinese doctor's face I like and a raccoon I like,
I hear a woman reciting numbers growing larger and larger
which I take as bad news – I think I see a turtle,
then on the surface an asp or coral snake.
One bite from a coral snake in Mexico,
you'll take a machete and cut off your arm
if you want to live. I would do that if it would help.

I say, 'It's a miracle.' The Chinese doctor and the moon
look down on me, and say silently, 'Who is this idiot?'
I tell myself, if I lie still enough I'll have a chance,
if I keep my eyes open they will not close forever.
I recall that Muhammad was born from a blood clot.
If I'm smiling, my smile must be like a scissors opening,
a knife is praying to a knife.
Little did I know, in a day, on a Walkman,
I would hear Mozart's second piano concerto,

that I would see a flock of Canada geese flying south
down the East River past the smokestacks of Long Island City.
I had forgotten the beauty in the world. I remember. I remember.

Bernard O'Donoghue

The Company of the Dead

It's natural that they would feel the cold
much more than we do; but that is partly
what makes them such good company.
They draw closer, rubbing their hands,
and praise the fire: 'That's a fine fire you've down.'

Also, they've no unrealised agendas,
their eager questions no barbed implications.
They're no trouble round the place, their only wish
now to get warmer: apart, that is, from wishing
that they'd kept warmer while they had the chance.

Dennis O'Driscoll

Out of Control

Worry on, mothers: you have
good reason to lose sleep,
to let imaginations run riot
as you lie in bed, not counting sheep
but seeing sons and daughters
like lambs led to slaughter
in the road kill of Friday nights.

Remain on standby, mothers –
you never know your luck –
for the knock that would break
the silence like the shock
of a metallic impact against brick.
Keep imagining a police beacon,
a blue moon shattering the darkness.

Lie warily, mothers, where,
eighteen years before, conception
took place in the black of night,
a secret plot; wait restlessly,
as if for a doctor's test,
to find out whether
you are still with child.

Sharon Olds

First Hour

That hour, I was most myself. I had shrugged
my mother slowly off, I lay there
taking my first breaths, as if
the air of the room was blowing me
like a bubble. All I had to do
was go out along the line of my gaze and back,
out and back, on gravity's silk, the
pressure of the air a caress, smelling on my
self her creamy blood. The air
was softly touching my skin and tongue,
entering me and drawing forth the little
sighs I did not know as mine.
I was not afraid. I lay in the quiet
and looked, and did the wordless thought,
my mind was getting its oxygen
direct, the rich mix by mouth.
I hated no one. I gazed and gazed,
and everything was interesting, I was
free, not yet in love, I did not
belong to anyone, I had drunk
no milk, yet – no one had
my heart. I was not very human. I did not
know there was anyone else. I lay
like a god, for an hour, then they came for me,
and took me to my mother.

Don Paterson

Waking with Russell

Whatever the difference is, it all began
the day we woke up face-to-face like lovers
and his four-day-old smile dawned on him again,
possessed him, till it would not fall or waver;
and I pitched back not my old hard-pressed grin
but his own smile, or one I'd rediscovered.
Dear son, I was *mezzo del' cammin*
and the true path was as lost to me as ever
when you cut in front and lit it as you ran.
See how the true gift never leaves the giver:
returned and redelivered, it rolled on
until the smile poured through us like a river.
How fine, I thought, this waking amongst men!
I kissed your mouth and pledged myself forever.

Justin Quinn

WE EAT AT REZ'S...

We eat at Rez's, Covent Garden,
up-market Italian, but not outré.
Our waiter acts as though he's starred in
some West End hit for which we three
weren't even called in to audition.
But he's OK, and the mussel dish an
amazing mix of delicate tastes.
We tell old stories, mock Jack's waist,
Shane's vanity and my spud haircut.
The digs and banter leave unmentioned
the legal separation. Our ancient
family house going on the market.
Lost in space. Our childhood shrinks,
but flows in coloured hyperlinks.

Christopher Reid

Bollockshire

You've zoomed through it often enough
on the long grind north, the grim dash south –
  why not take a break?
  Slip off the motorway
at any one of ten tangled junctions
and poke your nose, without compunction,
  into the unknown.
  Get systematically lost.
At the first absence of a signpost,
opt for the least promising lane,
  or cut into the truck traffic
  along some plain,
perimeter-fence-lined stretch of blacktop
heading nowhere obvious.
  Open your mind
  to the jarring yellow
of that hillside rape crop, the grim Norse green
of that fir plantation, where every tree
  steps forward to greet you
  with the same zombie gesture
of exclamation, the last-ditch brown of –
what could it be? Something to do with pigs?
  Row on row
  of miniature Nissen huts
laid out like a new speculative estate
in acres of glistening mud, behind an electronic gate...
  But don't stop now.
  Press on,
undistracted by the lush hedgerows
(of which there are none)
  or the silence of the songbirds.
  Other counties
can match these. It's the essence of Bollockshire

you're after: its secrets, its blessings and bounties.
    So keep driving,
        past sly-windowed farms,
lying there with hoards of costly machinery
in their arms, like toys they won't share;
        past Bald Oak Hill,
            down the more shaded side of which
the Bollockshire Hunt has scuffled
many a morning to its kill;
        past St Boldric's church,
            with the slant steeple,
which Cromwell's lads once briefly visited,
leaving behind them saints re-martyred,
        the Virgin without her head;
            past Bewlake Manor's
dinky Gothic gatehouse, now the weekend habitat
of London media or money people;
        past the isolated
            Bulldog pub,
with its choice of scrumpies, microwave grub,
bouncy castle and back-room badger fights –
        past all that,
            until, if you are lucky,
you hit the famous ring road. Thrown down
decades ago, like a gigantic concrete garland
        around the county town,
            riddled and plugged
by the random dentistry of maintenance work
and chock-a-block with contraflow,
        it must, you feel,
            be visible from the moon.
One road sign hides another. There are orange cones
galore. Each cultivated roundabout island
        is, if possible, more off-key
            than the one before.
But don't stick here all afternoon:
Blokeston itself has to be seen,

        via the brick maze
        of its bygone industrial outskirts.
This is where Silas Balk invented his machine
for putting a true, tight twist in string,
        where they once supplied the world
        with all it needed
of bicycle saddles and cigarette papers,
where cough syrup was king.
        Round the corner
        just when you least expect,
there's Blokeston FC, home of 'The Blockers',
and Blokeston Prison, by the same no-frills architect.
        Unmissable from any position,
        the Bulwark Brewery
stands up in a haze of its own malty vapours,
which even today's counterwafts of tandoori
        cannot contest.
        Now, turn east or west,
and you'll find yourself on a traffic-planner's
one-way inward spiral, passing at speed
        through older and older
        parts of town –
the impeccable Georgian manners
of Beauclerc Square, built on slave-trade money;
        bad Bishop Bloggs's school;
        the crossroads where
the Billhook Martyrs were tortured and burned –
until you reach the river Bleak.
        Squeeze, if you can,
        over the Black Bridge,
then park and pay – assuming this isn't the week
of the Billycock Fair, or Boiled Egg Day,
        when they elect the Town Fool.
        From here, it's a short step
to the Bailiwick Hall Museum and Arts Centre.
As you enter, ignore the display
        of tankards and manacles, the pickled head

          of England's Wisest Woman;
ask, instead, for the Bloke Stone.
Surprisingly small, round, featureless,
          pumice-grey,
          there it sits, dimly lit,
behind toughened glass, in a room of its own.
Be sure to see it, if you've a taste
          for this sort of primitive conundrum.
          Most visitors pass
and won't even leave their vehicles,
keen by this time to make haste
          back to the life they know,
          and to put more motorway under them.

Carol Rumens

Pledge to the Freight Canvasser

I'll take you with me when I board the ship
And if the ship turns out to be a boat,
The boat, a raft, the raft, a tattering branch
Flung from a boy's seaside story, tethered
At once to every whim that shakes the rootless ocean,
I'll stow your name, I'll roll it tinier than
Your shyest signature, and we'll be snug,
Low in the water, singing as we have to,
As ever targeted and separated
Children of the war. With hands and knees
Wrapped tight around our names, we'll sail together
Until the ocean tires and there's an orchard:
And if the orchard's just a single fruit tree
And if the fruit tree is a single branch,
And if the branch has only one good blossom
It will be yours, to form you always, when
I leave your name, there, warrior, underneath your ship.

Ann Sansom

Vehicle

Tomorrow, you'll be told this car is lethal.
Even the mechanic will back off from it;
the wishbone almost snapped, the engine bouncing
loose at every turn, a miracle it's not dropped out
on the road to Langsett Barn.

But tonight, you reach for the green-lit dash,
turn up the radio for a violin and flutes
and the baby a week from birth obliges us,
raising her knees, pedalling against my ribs.
Warm at last, we ease out of scarves

and take the long way to see where it leads.
The new city rewinds on the dark, returns us
to miles of slick steep road, snow swilled off fields,
dark villages we coast through, in no hurry.
In the back, our eldest nurses an axe,

hoping for difficult logs. Either side of him
the others jostle, elbow for space.
Firstborn is never a fortunate position.
They envy him the axe, the earring,
his silence. He endures them.

They'll learn. Eventually, they'll learn
responsibility. The weight of being trusted
with a weapon. Hard work. Decision.
Up front, we give up on the map,
let the headlights bring us out, at last.

Hagg Hill, Bolderstone, a dozy owl,
until a grind of gears and, dropping down,
we make the turn for Langsett woods.

We slide on mulch and frozen stone,
duck under branches, filing down to where
the res shifts smoke inside the boundary wall
not water at all though the trees sound like a sea
of needles and branches, breaking on remnants
of leaves and grubby sky. The children work,
their gloves slimy with sodden bark
and I, unbalanced and idle, wedge myself
in a system of knuckled roots and wait.
Here, I'm all agreement, gifted with children

and a minute's peace. I want for nothing,
no miracles aside from this. Home,
we'll tip the spoils out on the hearth,
reprieve this one with the snout and mane,
a beaten horse, and burn without compassion

the spiny rest, wanting warmth. We talk
on the road back, while the car labours and protests
then relaxes on the downslopes, at speed.
The kids sleep. Behind the wipers, secure
and warm, we're rocked almost into sleep.

Joe Sheerin

CEREMONIES

I hate preliminaries,
grace before meals, lipping
the wine and smelling the cork,

Kissing before love-
making, small talk before kissing,
pregnancy before childbirth,
childhood before the real thing.

Arguing before the big bust-up,
manoeuvres before the shooting war.

I hate the bit players before
the main actor, the failed comedian
before the funny man, the chorus
girls before the stripper, the clown
before the tightrope walker,
the triple jump before the high wall,
the ball boys before the players,
the umpire before the bowler
and the damned music before everything.

Most of all I hate long drawn out
illness, praying and drugtaking,
mending and regressing, ingrown
tears and fake jollity

when one could simply drop
dead in the middle of something.

Jean Sprackland

LOSING THE DARK

November, when day should close early
like a dull book. But that afternoon
a small cloud in the shape of a question-mark
passed over the sun and dissolved.
Six o'clock; eight; ten. Daylight
still flooded the startled street.

Such a gift. Like one of those summer evenings
when you sit out, glass in hand,
under the darting flightpaths of swifts.
It opened faces, shops, back doors.
Sleep and secrets were like dusty fetishes;
we took midnight walks, made love in sunlit rooms.
Even on the seventh night, dreamless
and nervy, we couldn't foresee it:

this shoving and kicking for basements
and underground stations, away from the glare
that opens you like a knife. How all the birds
might sing themselves to death.

Anne Stevenson

NEW YORK IS CRYING

New York is crying. I didn't hear screaming, just dead, dark silence.
Tyrone Dux, New York policeman, quoted in The Observer *(London),*
16 September 2001

Halfmast New York is crying for her children.
Her firemen, her policemen, her bagwomen,
Her smart investment analysts, her crooks,
Her execuwives in Gucci scarves and pantsuits,
Her TV chatterers and glossy-skinned presenters,
Her cleaners, waitresses and fast food cooks,
Her manicured secretaries and stubby-fingered punters,
Crying because they didn't die or scream.

Her preachers, her evangelists, her health cranks,
Her good-time girls and crack-addicts, her muggers,
Her Italian-Irish-Jewish politicians,
Her lawyers, paralegals and illegals,
Her internet whiz-kids and computer freaks,
Her trouble-shooters, paranoids, beauticians,
Deli proprietors, winos, hot musicians,
Dames with purple hair and crimson poodles...
Listen to them crying, but not screaming.

Is that Walt Whitman? Yes, but he is crying.
Hart Crane, in tears, is haunting Brooklyn Bridge.
Wystan, Dr Williams, mr cummings,
Miss Moore, Miss Bishop, look, they have come flying
In clouds of etymology, but crying.
Even John Astor and Henry Frick are trying,
Under the brassy marble of their monuments,
To sympathise with people who are dying.
Old Teddy Roosevelt, high on your moral horse,
What bracing words can dignify such crying?

But now a Mayor with a bedside manner,
And now a President in shining armour
Weep in the lens light of a billion eyes.
They want the world to notice they are crying.
Tears shall be sown in steel like dragon's teeth.
A crop of planes will pulverise the skies
While terrorists in terror cringe beneath.
Downtown, the bagel man on Chambers Street
Plasters his cart with frantic stars and stripes.
One wild-eyed Rasta with a bongo beats
Implacable voodoos under pulsing lights.
Flowers in the chainlink barrier are dying.

The ghostdust sours and settles with its smell
Of sulphurous flesh, stench of a Polish pit
Old Zbigniew Mirsky, eighty, knows too well;
One sniff, and his tower of hope falls into it.
The architect, America, was lying.
And here's the paper shop of Nizam Din
Locked behind shattered glass. No one's buying
His colourful books or letting strangers in.
The hole in New York is a hole in a belief
That desperately needs to hide itself in grief…
Professor X is lecturing, not crying.
Now, desert scenes and bursts of golden fire.
Those ragged children scuttling here and there
Are very small and far away, but crying.

Jenny Swann

THE FINISHING TOUCHES

Although you are the last man in the world
to care if your shirts are ironed and starched
I iron them anyway –

in an archaic, some might say misguided,
act of devotion, I position the board
by the window and get up steam

as rain thrums on the garden
where tulips the colours of *Smarties*
balance themselves on implausibly long stems.

Sleeves and collar first as taught by women
blaze-flushed by the range, in days
before ironing shirts for men wasn't done;

then I run the cusped nose down the back
no-one will ever see (for as often
as not you keep your jacket on)

smooth the length of it to perfection,
remembering the unknown sculptors
working on the statues for the Parthenon,

who knew their marbles would face out
on the world from high on the temple,
yet nonetheless chose to carve the backs as well;

to put the finishing touches to drapery
billowing out behind Athena and Amphitrite,
the curls on the head of Apollo,

recognising deep inside themselves an ideal,
a sense of a job well done, albeit visible
to none but the gods and the swallows.

Charles Tomlinson

For T H

I caught today something that you'd once said.
It re-formed in the echo-chambers of the head
Bringing with it the voice of its saying
(Your voice) and even the atmosphere of a morning
On Hartland's cliffs and the steady pace that we
Kept up beside the murmurings of that sea.
It was the music of speech you were describing
And the way such sounds must either die or sing,
The satisfactions of speech being musical
When we talk together a man with no talent at all
For music in the matters of everyday
Stays tedious despite what he has to say –
Even on subjects that might wake one's fantasies,
For what we want is that exchange of melodies,
The stimulation of tunes that answer one another
In the salt and sway of the sea's own weather
As they did that day we faced into the wind there,
And now return in thought, so that I hear
The dance of the words, like verse itself, renew
The sounded lineaments of the world we move through.

Gregory Warren Wilson

High Rise Flat

Up here with binoculars I used to watch
small white packets change hands –
conjurers, palming. Then
they'd piss in coke tins on the footbridge
and cool down cyclists.
But knives… that's different.

So I went to the RSPCA, chose a manky scrap,
paws big as lily pads, and fed him up –
tinned soup, bacon rind, leftovers from the fridge.
To start with he'd wolf the lot, then be sick.

I taught him everything. Manners
and that; not to lick his balls
when I brought birds back.
He'd have jumped off the balcony
to retrieve the moon if I'd trained him to.

Only thing he never got the hang of
was the lifts. He liked them Out of Order.
Both of them.
He sussed that one was for the odd floors
(no good to us) but whenever I dived in the other
he'd follow all right.

If I slithered out just as the doors shut
he'd be trapped like a cockroach in a matchbox;
by the time they opened automatically I'd have legged it
halfway up to the 12th floor. He'd chase,
slavering, straight from hell. Drove him mad.

Sometimes I'd press the wrong button,
all innocent, and wait.

Soon as we arrived he knew something was up,
but couldn't tell which way to jump.
I'd make a dash, then halt

and watch him lollop up or down a flight, stop,
wheel round…
There were times on the landing
when he'd look me in the eye and growl
before I'd even made a move.

He had other ways of getting me back;
streetwise, he'd pull one leg after the other.

Matthew Welton

Dozen

the thoughts flustering like the wind around these gardens
                                        overlooking the sea
the thoughts these children described with a fingers-in-a-hornet-
                                        hole kind of a hubbub

the thoughts we went through that first summer of the
                                        grasshopper-fever epidemic
the thoughts the girl in the tennis-dress was anxious to make
                                        understood

those thoughts coming out in tangles as we sat together in silence
the thoughts we got onto as we hurried out to the roof

the thoughts taking shape as we queued silently for pastries this
                                        morning
the thoughts communicated by an abrupt or showy quickening of
                                        the breath

the thoughts we went into over that supper of artichokes and
                                        spaghetti
the thoughts expanded upon in *chaoticism and opportunity in the
                                        indian raj*

the thoughts copied out into the fly-leaves of the *contemporary
                                        colorists year-book*
the thoughts wafting through the mind like this lemons-and-
                                        burned-sugar kind of smell

the thoughts muddling around the mind like the shadows inside
                                        our room
the thought of a fat man speaking quietly with a thin man

the thoughts set out in later editions of *the daubist movement*
manifesto
the thoughts which make their visit during these closing moments
of sleep

the thoughts spoken into a telephone outside a room somewhere
in iraq
the thoughts we discuss over lunch, a little drunken on
hickory-flavour beer

these thoughts taking shape as a slow yellow sunlight thickens the
windows
that thought which yesterday came to us as we were driving west

the thought involved in remembering why it was we ever left
honolulu
the thoughts dismantled like bicycle-parts one idle spring morning
around tel aviv

the thoughts borrowed from the books we found sunning in the
window
the thoughts we recollect from our afternoons of frantic and
loving sex

these thoughts like clouds that lie like dead dogs in the sky
these thoughts which translate into a feverish low-pitched melodic
kind of buzz